The OTHER side of the COIN™

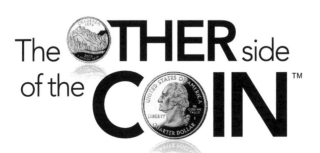

Compound Interest
10 Financial Truths to Protect Your Wealth

Copyright © 2016 by Will Duffy

WWW.VERITY.FINANCIAL

First Edition

Includes bibliographical references.

ISBN13: 978-1534606401

ISBN10: 1534606408

I. Business—Investing II. Duffy, Will III. Title

Cover design by Brad Haima, CircleGraphics.ca

Interior design & typesetting by Colleen Sheehan, WDRBookdesign.com

The OTHER side of the COIN™

COMPOUND INTEREST

10 Financial Truths to Protect Your Wealth

Will Duffy, ChFC

ACKNOWLEDGMENTS

I CAN'T IMAGINE the path to success in any venture without a mentor. Mentors are invaluable, yet their job often seems thankless. When it comes to making progress, a mentor almost literally transfers time. Experience takes time, usually years, and mentors can transfer their experience in a moment.

I am extremely grateful to have had in my career not just *a* mentor, but many mentors. The least I can do is acknowledge them for their time, dedication, commitment, and willing heart to transfer to me their knowledge and experience.

Seven men and women listed below have helped me reach the point I am at today. Thank you!

Bryan Bloom, CPA
Ed Slott, CPA
Jeff Webb
Kim Butler
Todd Langford
Tom Love
Van Mueller

CONTENTS

FINANCIAL ADVISOR Will Duffy shatters the myths of compound interest that so many have relied on as financial gospel. Most people know that compound interest means exponential growth over the long term, and that's especially good for savers. But many savers who count on this concept are not reaping the full benefit due to several substantial roadblocks. The two biggest are taxes and market risk, which not only stunt growth, but can actually reverse it, sending you in the wrong direction. Imagine driving backward on your road to retirement. That's the wrong direction!

Will's *10 Financial Truths* expose the major practical flaws in the theory of compound interest. Now you can recognize them when you see them—and change direction. This is the first step toward receiving consistent positive returns over time. This is where true long-term financial security begins.

Ed Slott, CPA
Retirement expert
Founder of *www.irahelp.com*
March 1, 2016

WHAT JUST AIN'T SO

"It ain't what you don't know that gets you in trouble.
It's what you know for sure that just ain't so."
—Mark Twain

MARK TWAIN could have been speaking about financial security and retirement when he made those remarks. As a financial advisor, it's painful for me to see how many people accept as gospel all kinds of so-called truths that, in Twain's words, "just ain't so."

Bad information consistently flows from a wide variety of seemingly reputable sources, including some widely recognized financial authorities as well as major financial institutions and government agencies.

Within the world of big finance, a host of interests and motivations influences the distribution of information. Even if each of these interests operates with the best intentions, their messages become distorted by a handful of persistent myths.

In some areas of life, myths may be quaint and harmless. But financial security isn't one of them. When it comes time to retire, learning you'd put your trust in widely held truths "that just ain't so" would be devastating.

I've seen this devastation up close, and it's heartbreaking.

James, a man in his late fifties, came into my office. He was clearly distressed. I asked him what's going on.

"I'm looking at this Retirement Readiness Report you prepared for me, and something's wrong. You're telling me my 401(K), which has a balance of $1 million, will provide only $30,000 per year for us to live on. I don't believe it. It can't be right!"

I reminded him that at retirement, the entire 401(K)—both contributions and gains—is subject to federal and state income taxes.

Before I could continue, James jumped in. "It still doesn't add up. I maxed out my 401(K) contributions at work for most of my career. When I had to withdraw funds for a couple emergencies, I paid back every cent to my 401(K). I thought I was doing all the right things. The rate of return was pretty good most of the time. What went wrong?"

He looked down at the floor. "I don't know what I'm going to do. We can't live on this. We just can't. There goes the lake home. And so much for travel to Europe and New Zealand. And what about the grandkids? I always dreamed we'd be able to help them with college." James dropped his head into his hands. "How did I let this happen?"

As James and I sat there in silence, I thought, *How does this keep happening to people like James? These are good people who are trying to be responsible with their finances.*

Our first impulse on hearing sad stories like James's is to assume they're an isolated case. We really don't want to face this horrible truth: Today it's more the exception than the rule that

TODAY IT'S MORE THE EXCEPTION THAN THE RULE THAT PEOPLE HAVE AMPLE SAVINGS AND WILL ONE DAY BE ABLE TO RETIRE COMFORT-ABLY—OR EVEN RETIRE AT ALL.

people have ample savings and will one day be able to retire com-fortably—or even retire at all.

Let that sink in and you'll realize you can't wait another day to separate the fantasy from reality when it comes to your finan-cial security.

In this series, I cut to the chase on the subjects that matter most to your financial wellbeing. These lessons and insights have turned things around for my clients—and I'm confident they'll make a difference for you as well.

If you're willing to consider the other side of the coin, the truth really will set you free.

COMPOUND
INTEREST

10 Financial Truths to
Protect Your Wealth

WHAT EINSTEIN KNEW

WHY DO we invest our money? Because we want that money to grow. And why do we want our money to grow? Because then we'll have more money! It's a simple concept. Money locked in a safe or stashed under a mattress will never grow into more. But when that money is invested, our goal is to have it turn into more money.

This is such a simple concept. But does the average saver and investor really understand the ins and outs of having their money grow?

To seek out the answer, let's start with some familiar information. We've all heard about the power of compound interest.

We may have been told that compound interest is magic. Someone may have called it a miracle. It's reported that Albert Einstein referred to compound interest as "the Eighth Wonder of the World." Einstein felt so strongly about the power of compound interest, he's claimed to have said, "He who understands it, earns it … he who doesn't … pays it."

Join me in learning ten financial truths about compound interest. You won't need to be an Einstein to understand them—or profit from them.

ONE OF THE GREATEST TOOLS FOR BUILDING WEALTH

COMPOUND INTEREST sure sounds like a great thing. But let's take it a bit further. Some of this information will probably be familiar. Even if the examples you've heard might be slightly different, the concept remains the same.

To demonstrate the power of compound interest, consider this mental experiment: You get to choose whether to receive one million dollars today or one penny that's doubled every day for the next thirty days.

What would you choose? Almost everyone is quick to choose the million dollars. A bird in the hand is worth two in the bush.

Because you are the inquisitive type (after all, you're reading this book), you might ask for more information before you make your choice. You might want to know what a single penny has grown to after one week. The answer is a whopping sixty-four cents.

You might further ask what the penny has grown to after two weeks. There's a lot more than just sixty-four cents. The penny, doubled every day, has now grown to $81.92.

Not to push your luck too far, you decide to ask one more question to guide you to make the right decision. Your final question is how much the doubled penny is worth after three weeks. The answer is $10,485.76.

That's still a far cry from the million dollars. So with confidence you decide you'll take the million dollars—after obtaining what you feel is enough information to make an informed choice.

So what was the right choice? The million dollars—or the penny doubled for thirty days? I'm sure you've already figured out that I'll tell you the penny. You're right. While this is shocking to most, the most-shocking part is how much that penny has grown by day thirty.

Are you sitting down? A penny doubled every day for thirty days would grow to more than five million dollars! ($5,368,709.12, in fact.) If you don't believe me, grab your calculator and come back to the book in five minutes.

The number is astounding. Unfortunately, investing a penny that will double every day for thirty days is not something we can do. But there's a lesson here. That lesson is the power, magic, or miracle of compound interest.

THE MOST BASIC DEFINITION OF COMPOUND INTEREST IS WHEN YOU EARN INTEREST ON BOTH YOUR PRINCIPAL AND YOUR INTEREST.

No matter what we decide to call it, let's be honest. There isn't any magic involved. And this is definitely not a miracle. So what's the secret?

The secret, if you will, lies in the definition of compound interest.

The most basic definition of compound interest is when you earn interest on both your principal *and* your interest. This is different from simple interest, where interest is earned only on the principal. When interest can be earned on both principal and interest, big things happen. There is a snowball effect that brings big gains over time as both your principal and your earned interest combine.

FINANCIAL TRUTH #1
COMPOUND INTEREST IS ONE OF THE GREATEST TOOLS FOR BUILDING WEALTH.

What does the snowball effect of compound interest mean for you? If you have ever entered into an investment, you probably were shown some numbers to help you picture what your investment might look like at a given time in the future.

These numbers may have been in the form of a prospectus, an illustration, or just a projection on a spreadsheet. You may have done some calculating yourself because it's fun to see what the fruits of our labor could produce one day. These figures demonstrate compound interest.

If you have $100,000 to invest, you might be shown that $100,000 invested for 30 years at 8% annual interest will grow to over one million dollars. ($1,006,265.69 to be exact.) Or maybe you want to start contributing to your company's retirement plan, and you decide you would like to contribute $10,000 every year to the plan. $10,000 contributed annually for 30 years at 8% annual interest would also grow to over one million dollars. (That's $1,223,458.68 for the detailed folks like myself.) Sounds like a no-brainer. But is it?

Unfortunately, many factors over 30 years will get between us and that million dollars. While these numbers are mathematically correct, they are only part of the truth.

Are you okay with that? Or do you want the whole truth? I passionately believe everyone deserves to know the whole truth about how wealth really works. That is why my company is called Verity Financial, because *verity* means truth. So as broadcaster Paul Harvey would say, let's look at the rest of the story.

The biggest truth we are never told is that to achieve the true power of compound interest, nothing can be allowed to interrupt the growth. And I mean *nothing*. As soon as there's an interruption, even a small one, all bets are off. The results are dramatically different.

What kind of interruptions am I talking about? Let me give you a few of the many possible examples. These include investment losses, account fees, taxes on gains, and purchases made with the invested money.

THE BIGGEST TRUTH WE ARE NEVER TOLD
IS THAT TO ACHIEVE THE TRUE POWER
OF COMPOUND INTEREST, NOTHING CAN BE
ALLOWED TO INTERRUPT THE GROWTH. AS
SOON AS THERE'S ANY INTERRUPTION, ALL
BETS ARE OFF.

INVESTMENT LOSSES. This is simply when your asset declines in value. A stock you own might drop in price and even be worth less than you paid for it.

ACCOUNT FEES. These are costs associated with investing. You might have to pay a mutual fund fee if you are invested in a particular fund. Or there could be a fee for management that an advisor charges to manage your accounts.

TAXES ON GAINS. A tax is something the government assesses to the gains in your investments. This could be a capital gains tax associated with a long-term gain in your investment.

PURCHASES MADE WITH INVESTED MONEY. Finally, you may liquidate all or part of your investment to make a purchase. These could be almost anything, but common large purchases include buying a car, putting a down payment on a house, or responding to a financial emergency.

WHAT'S POSSIBLE?

Before we look at the impact that interruptions can have on the compound growth of our money, let me ask you a question: Do you think it's possible to earn uninterrupted compound growth? Is it possible to never have any interruptions, including those I just listed?

The answer is probably no. And if we cannot earn compound interest without any type of interruption, does that mean all of the projections we've looked at are invalid? The answer is probably yes.

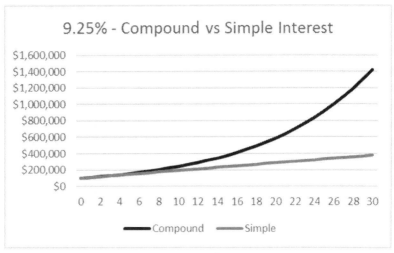

Figure 1[1]

A picture is worth a thousand words, so in Figure 1 you'll find a representation of what the compound interest curve looks like. For comparison's sake, the graph also includes simple interest.

[1] The 9.25% interest is not arbitrary. This is the S&P 500 (with dividends) average return for the past 19 years (1997–2015).

The first thing you may notice is that the compound interest curve is not linear, meaning it's not a straight line. The simple interest line, however, is linear. At first the two lines are close. But after a few years, the compound interest curve takes off. With time, the real magic happens. (All graphs in this book start out with $100,000 and no additional contributions.)

THE EFFECT OF INVESTMENT LOSSES

What happens when something interrupts this curve? Let's start by looking at losses. Losses are something most people expect to have occasionally in their investments. For illustration purposes, I cherry-picked a time when the stock market averaged a rate of return of approximately 9%. I chose the S&P 500 (including dividends), from 1997 to 2015. This is a period of 19 years when this index averaged a gain of 9.25%. Not bad!

Let's start by calculating the results of $100,000 invested for 19 years at a true uninterrupted compound interest rate of 9.25%. The account balance at the end of 19 years, as shown in Figure 2, would be $537,041.[2]

As you can see, if we deposited $100,000 into an account and that account grew by a compounded 9.25% every year, at the end of 19 years we would have $540,000. That's more than half a million dollars! Surely we would end up with the same dollar figure if we invested in the stock market, if the market returned an average of 9.25% over 19 years, right? Let's take a look.

---

2   Hereafter, $537,041 will be rounded to $540,000.

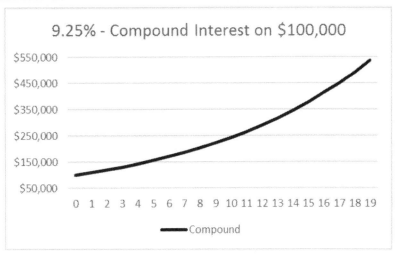

Figure 2

If we had invested $100,000 into the S&P 500 and let it grow from 1997 to 2015, averaging a 9.25% return over those 19 years, as shown in Figure 3, our balance at the end of the 19 years would be just $392,307.[3] That puts us almost $145,000 short from the $540,000 to which we anticipated our account growing.

How can this be? All the variables were the same. The deposit amount was the same. The time span of 19 years was the same. And the rate of return in both scenarios was 9.25%. So what gives?

There is one key difference between the two scenarios, and that difference is *losses*.

In the first example, there was never a loss. For 19 years straight, the return was a consistent, positive 9.25%. But in the second example, that of investing in stocks, during the 19-year period there were four years of losses. These interrupted our compound interest curve.

---

[3]   Hereafter, $392,307 will be rounded to $390,000.

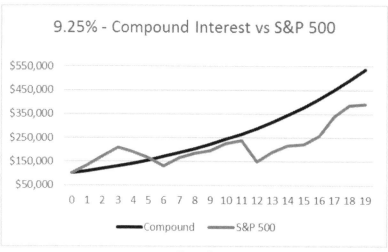

Figure 3

When we experience a loss, we lose our momentum. And when we lose our momentum, before we can continue to make any progress, we must work to get back to where we were. Our snowball loses a chunk of snow and has to gather new snow just to regain the missing piece. Let that word picture sink in for a moment. Not until the snowball replaces the missing snow, can it get back to where it *already was* and start to grow again.

TWO

WHEN LOSS HAPPENS

FINANCIAL TRUTH #2:
COMPOUND INTEREST STOPS COMPOUNDING WHEN
A LOSS IS EXPERIENCED.

I WANT TO make sure we are all on the same page. Though in our S&P scenario there were four losses in the 19-year period, the entire period still averaged 9.25%. Six of the 19 years had returns of over 20%. And two of those six years had a return of over 30%!

We are often told that to achieve the big gains, we need to expose ourselves to losses. Is that true? Ask yourself one question: With what we've covered so far, would you rather receive a consistent 9.25% each year or experience some losses for the ability to occasionally experience returns as high as 20% and even 30%?

I bet you $145,000 that I know which one you would now pick!

A popular children's story beautifully demonstrates what is going on here. It's one of Aesop's fables, called "The Tortoise and the Hare." We all remember this classic tale. A tortoise, tired of a hare's boasting, challenges him to a race. What chance does a turtle have? The hare, confident in his ability to win, leaves the tortoise in the dust. He gains such a lead and because he cannot lose, he decides it's okay to take a nap midway.

Meanwhile the tortoise starts the race and continues with the same steady pace. He is consistent. He does not stop or slow. When the hare awakes, he hears cheers from those at the finish line, celebrating the tortoise's victory. Slow and steady wins the race.

Does this translate to investing? Absolutely. Consistent returns can win the race—over the up and down returns of traditional financial thinking.

The bottom line is this: If you do not receive consistent positive returns in your account, you will not end up with the same amount of money a compound interest calculation says you will. Even if you average the same rate of return that the compound interest calculator used to calculate your growth, you will end up with less money.

Let's look at this from a different perspective. You would have to earn only 7.46% interest consistently on your $100,000 for 19 years to end up with the same $390,000 that resulted from being invested in the stock market from 1997 to 2015. That means you lost almost two percentage points from your return—just by adding losses into the mix.

THE EFFECT OF FEES

Let's continue with these same numbers and add another interruption that destroys the power of compounding. This time it's fees.

Are there fees associated with your investments? You bet there are. No one can avoid fees, especially when investing in the stock market. Even day traders must pay for their trades. But since most of us are not day traders, we incur additional fees. These might come in the form of a management fee, a mutual fund fee, or the costs associated with buying and selling stocks and bonds.

The total amount someone pays in investment-related fees can vary significantly. Some people might pay as little as under 2% annually, while others' fees might be as high as over 4%. In an article in *Forbes* on "The Real Cost of Owning a Mutual Fund," [4] Ty Bernicke states the average cost of owning a mutual fund is 3.17% per year. But let's be optimistic and use 2%.

The next chapter lays out the consequences.

4 www.forbes.com/2011/04/04/real-cost-mutual-fund-tax-es-fees-retirement-bernicke.html

THREE

FEES ARE YOUR FOE

FINANCIAL TRUTH #3:

COMPOUND INTEREST STOPS COMPOUNDING WHEN
A FEE IS CHARGED TO OUR ACCOUNT.

SO WHAT happens to your compounding interest as fees are
taken out of your account balances each year? For starters, consider that a fee is very similar to a loss. Let's be honest; it *is* a loss.
It might be a minor one, but it's still a loss.

And this loss will be slightly different from a market loss. Any
guesses about the nature of that difference?

This loss happens *every* year. In the example for Financial
Truth #2, in the s&p 500 from 1997 to 2015, there were only four
years with losses. But fees are charged *every single year*. So while
these losses might appear small, they are consistent. That means
they are a constant interruption in the compounding of our investment.

Adding losses to the mix brought our projected account balance from $540,000 down to $390,000. If we add 2% in annual fees for those 19 years, as shown in Figure 4, the growth in the investment drops from $390,000 to $267,252.[5]

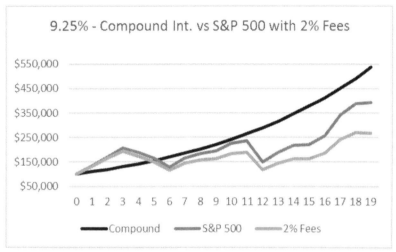

Figure 4

That's quite a hit! We lost almost $145,000 when we added losses to the picture, and now we've lost another $125,000. That's a combined $270,000 reduction from what we would have received if our compound interest had no interruptions.

I will go into more depth on fees and their effect on our investments in a future book in my The Other Side of the Coin series, but I want to briefly highlight a fascinating (and devastating) discovery I made. Yet before I do, I want to make sure you are clear about what just happened with the 2% in annual fees.

[5]   Hereafter, $267,252 will be rounded to $270,000.

We did not pay $125,000 in fees. But our account value dropped $125,000 from what it would have grown to without the annual fees. So where is the rest of the money? The answer lies in this discovery.

WHERE DID THE MONEY GO?

When our accounts grow because the stock market experiences a gain, we do not get to fully realize that gain because of the fees we must pay. If the stock market returns 10% one year, our account would not match the 10% growth—once the fees are paid out of our account. (Yes, fees could be paid from other money outside of our investments, but the result would be the same. That other money could be invested, and over time the lost opportunity cost would represent the same loss we are discussing here.)

Those fees we pay, associated with our investments, reduce their growth. And over time, the reduction is dramatic.

Check again for the reduction seen in Figure 4. As you notice the increase that happens in years 1 and 2, you'll see that the line that represents the stock market growth is above the line that represents our investment in the stock market *with fees*.

This shows that our gain will always be less than the stock market gain because fees are taken out of our account. So you will never do as well as the stock market does when the stock market goes up. While I found this discovery fascinating, you can start to see why it's also devastating. But it actually gets more riveting—and more devastating.

What happens when the stock market declines? The loss we experience in our account value is always worse than the stock market's decline!

That's right. This is a lose-lose situation. First, our accounts do not experience the full gain the stock market does. Second, when the stock market goes down, our account's loss is actually *worse*. Again, look at Figure 4. Years 4 through 6 have losses. Notice that the line that represents the stock market lies above the line that represents our investment in the stock market with fees. So we actually experience a worse loss than the stock market itself.

Our gains are not as good—and our losses are worse! Intriguing? For sure. Devastating? Absolutely. And there's more.

This pattern has its own compounding effect. And this compounding effect is always negative because it reduces what our account would have grown to without fees. Further, because of fees the gap between the stock market returns and our actual account values will continue to widen over the course of our investment. Go back to Figure 4 one more time. Notice the stock market line and the stock market with fees line start with a paper thin gap. But by the time you get to year 19, the gap is so big, it represents a difference of over $125,000! And if we were to continue the graph even longer, say 30 years, the gap would continue to expand.

BECAUSE OF FEES, WE CAN'T DO AS WELL AS THE STOCK MARKET EVEN WHEN IT'S UP, AND WE DO WORSE THAN THE STOCK MARKET WHEN IT'S DOWN.

This discovery really opened my eyes to the significance that fees have on suppressing how much money an account can accrue. Not until I really studied the graph did I notice this growth reduction was due to the fact that our gains are lessened by fees—and our losses are made worse by fees. Because of fees, we cannot do as well as the stock market even when it is up, and we do worse than the stock market when it is down.

As we did in the previous section, let's look at this again from a different angle. You would have to earn only 5.31% consistently, without losses or fees, to end up with the same $270,000. This means that because of losses and fees, our return has dropped from an average of 9.25% to an actual return of 5.31%. That's a drop of over 40%.

THE EFFECT OF TAXES

The next interruption we face is taxes. This is a big one. Taxes cannot be avoided. They can either be paid now or deferred, but not avoided. For this example, I'll assume our investment is not in a tax-deferred vehicle, such as a 401(K) or IRA. These accounts have limits, and you cannot contribute $100,000 into a 401(K) or IRA as we have discussed in our examples. Also, these 401(K) and IRA accounts will still be taxed, but not until later. Remember, *defer* is just a fancy word for postpone. I suspect few people would get as excited if these were called tax-postponement plans!

Taxation of investments gets complicated. There is different taxation based on the type of investment and how long it's held.

You might pay ordinary income tax on your gains, short-term capital gains tax, or long-term capital gains tax.

This section is not designed to explain the differences in taxes, only to show the effect taxes have on our compounding. To make things simple, I'll use a 15% tax rate. As of 2016 when this was written, this is one of the lowest long-term capital gains tax rates. Other long-term capital gains tax rates are 18.8%, 20%, and 23.8%. (These rates include the Net Investment Income Tax, which started in 2013.)

Currently, 15% also happens to be one of the lowest ordinary income tax rates. (Short-term capital gains rate is the same as the ordinary income tax rates.) Other ordinary income tax rates include 25%, 28%, 33%, 35%, and 39.6%. Translation: 15% is an extremely low tax rate.

So what do you think taxes will do to our compound growth? Once again, think of taxes as a loss. After all, they function just like a loss. When taxes are taken out of our account, our investment balance is reduced the same way it is with a loss or fee. Therefore, it will react the same way it did in the previous examples.

Let's state the obvious: The numbers will continue to go down. Interruptions in our compound growth never increase the account value. They always decrease it.

INTERRUPTIONS IN OUR COMPOUND GROWTH NEVER INCREASE THE ACCOUNT VALUE. THEY ALWAYS DECREASE IT.

FOUR

THE TAX MAN COMETH

FINANCIAL TRUTH #4:

COMPOUND INTEREST STOPS COMPOUNDING WHEN
TAXES ARE PAID ON OUR GAINS.

WE STARTED with a projection that having $100,000 invested at
a consistent interest rate of 9.25% would grow to $540,000 in 19
years. That number diminished to $390,000 when in the 19-year
period, our account experienced four losses. We still averaged a
9.25% return over that time, but four years with losses interrupted
our compounding curve, and the loss of momentum cannot be
fully regained. Our number decreased again due to fees, so we
now have just $270,000. (That means we are down to half of our
original $540,000 projection.) So now let's add Uncle Sam into
the mix, because one way or the other, he's going to get his money.

If we pay just 15% in taxes on our account in this example for the 15 years we had gains (we pay no taxes in the four years with losses), as shown in Figure 5, we end up with just $193,503.[6]

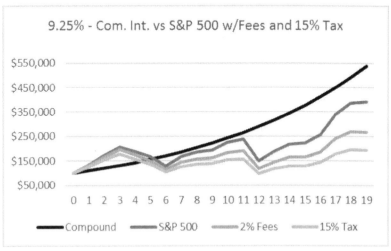

Figure 5

That's almost $75,000 in additional reduction of our account balance due to taxes. Looking at rates of return once again, you would need to earn just 3.54% consistently to end up with the same $190,000 you have with the interruptions of losses, fees,

ARE YOU STARTING TO SEE WHY YOUR PERSONAL INVESTMENTS ARE NOT WHERE YOU THOUGHT THEY'D BE?

6   Hereafter, $193,503 will be rounded to $190,000.

and taxes. Our actual return has dwindled to just about a third of 9.25%.

Are you starting to understand why your personal investments are not where you thought they would be at this stage in your life? Don't be discouraged. Knowledge is power. The truth will set you free. We're going to look at one more interruption.

FIVE

BORROWING FROM YOURSELF

THE EFFECT OF USING OUR OWN MONEY

THE FINAL interruption we will examine is something I call *life*. This might be the most important interruption to understand. *Life* happens to all of us. I'm speaking of both the expected and unexpected events that require a financial obligation.

For example, most of us would agree that an automobile is necessary in today's world. Cars cost money. So cars are an expected event that require a financial obligation.

Another great example is a house down payment. Buying a house is part of the American Dream, and unless you pay in full, one requirement to purchasing a house is a down payment. This amount is usually substantial, as houses are one of the largest purchases we ever make.

Or we face an unexpected financial emergency. This can be any number of things, but include needing to replace your car's transmission or your home's furnace, air conditioner, or water heater. Or you face unexpected medical bills.

So when life happens, what does that do to our compounding? Financially, it's pretty devastating—for two reasons. The first and most obvious reason is that like all other interruptions, it reduces our compound interest curve. In financial terminology, this is known as Lost Opportunity Cost, or LOC. When we take money out of our investments, even for a short time, we lose the gains that would have been made on that money. If we remove $10,000 from our account for one year and our account grew by 10%, we lost $1,000.

But that's not the only loss. We also lose what those lost gains would have grown to over time. We have lost the opportunity to earn interest on that money. The $1,000 that we lost would have continued to grow over time to some higher amount. So in reality we have lost not just $1,000, but also what that $1,000 would have grown to. This, again, is Lost Opportunity Cost.

The second reason it's so devastating, which people often miss or forget, is that this money is seldom put back. If we have the goal of putting $10,000 into an investment every year for 30 years so it will grow to over one million dollars, we cannot remove money and not put it back.

If we want to reach our goals, we still can use this money for those times when life happens. But we need to practice the discipline to return the money to our accounts—at least if we still want to reach that million dollars. Let's look at what happens when we remove money from our account for life events—and then actually put it back.

Here are some hypothetical life events and the resulting transactions that take place in our 19-year time period.

1. We buy a car for $10,000 at the beginning of year 2 and put the $10,000 back at the beginning of year 3.

2. We put a down payment of $30,000 on a house at the beginning of year 7 and put the $30,000 back at the beginning of year 9.

3. We need to upgrade our vehicle and buy a $20,000 vehicle at the beginning of year 9 and put the $20,000 back at the beginning of year 11.

4. We have a $15,000 emergency at the beginning of year 13 and put the $15,000 back at the beginning of year 15.

5. We need to upgrade our vehicle again and buy a $25,000 vehicle at the beginning of year 16 and put the $25,000 back at the beginning of year 18.

Before we look at what happens to our compounding interest due to these life interruptions, I want to make sure you understand what is happening. In the following figure, the exact dollar amounts that were taken out of the investment account to pay for these life events are being replaced at a future date. Now, how often do you think that happens in reality? Of course, it's extremely rare. But I want to make sure each of these graphs is a true apples-to-apples comparison. So in all of these calculations, the money is later returned to the account.

FINANCIAL TRUTH #5:
COMPOUND INTEREST STOPS COMPOUNDING WHEN WE USE OUR OWN MONEY.

When we factor just five life events into our compound interest curve, as shown in Figure 6, our account is now at just $156,428.[7]

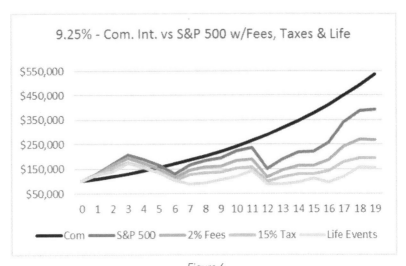

Figure 6

---

7   Hereafter, $156,428 will be rounded to $160,000.

Previously we had $190,000 after taxes, which means we just took another hit of more than $30,000 simply because we used our own money! Yes, the same amount of money was still deposited into the investment over the 19-year period. But because we dared to use our own hard-earned savings, we lost out.

RECALCULATING OUR GAINS

So one last time, let's look at this from the flipside and see what rate of return we would need to earn consistently to end up with the same amount of money after losses, fees, taxes, and life events. If your $100,000 earned just 2.38% on a true uninterrupted compound interest curve over 19 years, you would have the same $160,000.

So we have gone from thinking we would earn 9.25% each year—to ending up with the same amount of money we would have if we earned only 2.38%. As a direct result of interruptions, our interest rate has dropped by almost 75%. When life in all its forms happens, 9.25% shrinks to just 2.38%.

In the next chapter, we'll consider what we can do about that.

SIX

WHEN MORE ISN'T MORE

SO WHAT DO YOU DO?

LET'S QUICKLY SUMMARIZE, because I've given you a lot of information and a lot of numbers. When we first set out to obtain Einstein's Eighth Wonder of the World, compound interest, we calculated that if we earned 9.25% each year for 19 years straight, without any interruptions, our account would grow to $540,000. That means our cost basis (a fancy term for our contribution, excluding growth) is $100,000.

Had we ended up with $540,000, that would be $440,000 in growth! That's over four times what we put in. No wonder people call it a miracle.

But in reality, we ended up with a final account balance of just $160,000. Our growth went from almost $440,000 to under $60,000. That's about 90% less growth—a huge difference.

Do you feel like you're way behind where you thought you'd be at this point? I hope you now have an insight why.

With your newfound knowledge, you are probably wondering what actions you should take to prevent the interruptions we've discussed. I want to conclude by giving you some real solutions you can use in your own situation. I also want to encourage you in your pursuit of financial success and financial freedom.

ELIMINATING LOSSES

Let's start with our first interruption, losses. Is there anything you can do to eliminate losses in your investments? And the answer is a resounding yes. Today there are many financial vehicles that are not subject to the risk of losses. These simply never lose money.

Yes, these investment options are often downplayed because they do not have as high a rate of return as other options. Well, we now know that is not the whole story.

FINANCIAL TRUTH #6:
A HIGHER RATE OF RETURN DOES NOT ALWAYS RESULT IN MORE MONEY.

In the examples we've looked at, a 2.38% rate of return would result in the same account balance as a 9.25% average return with interruptions. So when we factor in all the variables, we discovered this astounding truth.

HIS FIRST RULE IS "NEVER LOSE MONEY." HIS SECOND IS "NEVER FORGET THE FIRST RULE."

It's mathematically possible—and more important, it's *realistically* possible—to end up with more money from a lower rate of return. The key is avoiding losses.

This principle is not my own discovery, nor is it something new. Warren Buffett, a man 53 years my senior and considered the world's most successful investor, has two rules for investing. His first rule is "Never lose money." His second rule is "Never forget the first rule."

There is true wisdom here. If you've never strongly considered eliminating all possibility of loss in your portfolio, I highly encourage you to do so. Remember, slow and steady won the race, and it still wins it—every time!

FACING DOWN FEES

Our next interruption was fees. Fees are the silent killer. And don't just take my word for it. Tony Robbins, in his book *MONEY Master the Game: 7 Simple Steps to Financial Freedom*[8], lists ten different fees being charged to investors and their investments.

If you want to be a successful investor, fees must be reduced or eliminated. This is a non-negotiable.

8   pp. 112–114

FINANCIAL TRUTH #7:
FEES CHARGED TO OUR ACCOUNT ARE A GUARANTEED REDUCTION IN OUR ACCOUNT VALUES.

Some will argue that higher fees might lead to higher returns. While that might be true in theory, we have seen the reality of what just 2% in annual fees does to our account balance.

Eliminating fees is a guaranteed win against the losses that fees create in our accounts. And again, many investment options today have little or no fees.

MANAGING TAXES

Up next is taxes. If you're thinking that I already said taxes can't be avoided, you're correct. But there's more to the story.

FINANCIAL TRUTH #8:
WE ARE NOT REQUIRED TO PAY TAXES ON OUR GAINS, IF WE USE SPECIFIC STRATEGIES THAT ARE APPROVED BY THE INTERNAL REVENUE CODE.

Taxes can't be avoided on your principal, but they can be eliminated (legally) on your gains. Let me say that again. Taxes cannot

TAXES CANNOT BE AVOIDED ON YOUR PRINCIPAL, BUT THEY CAN BE ELIMINATED ON YOUR GAINS.

be avoided on your principal, but they can be eliminated on your gains. This is *huge*.

Imagine again the ability to have $100,000 grow to $540,000 as we saw at the beginning. (That means $100,000 was your contribution and $440,000 was your growth.) Would you rather pay taxes on a $100,000 contribution or on $440,000 of gains? The answer is obvious. The ability to avoid taxes on your gains is a reality for most Americans, yet most fail to use this beneficial strategy.

Significantly, as CPA and tax advisor Ed Slott reminds us, there is a difference between tax avoidance and tax evasion. In his book *The Retirement Savings Tax Bomb... and How to Defuse It*, he says this in his section called "What's The Difference Between ...?":

> *Tax avoidance* is legal; *tax evasion* isn't. For example, this book will help you to *avoid* taxes, not evade them.[9]

EASING LIFE'S INTERRUPTIONS

Our last interruption is life. And no, I don't recommend you stop living! Our time on this planet is incredibly short.

---

[9] Ed Slott, The Retirement Savings Time Bomb... and How to Defuse It, p. 15.

My life felt like it went into hyperdrive when my wife and I had our first child in 2008. Where does time go when you have children? As I write this, my daughter Caelyn is 7, my son Gavin is 5, my son Weston is 2, and my wife is pregnant with Landon.

Before I know it, the kids will be out of the house and married with kids of their own. As the saying goes, today is a gift and that's why it's called the present.

FINANCIAL TRUTH #9:
LIFE INTERRUPTIONS DO NOT HAVE TO STOP OUR COMPOUNDING GROWTH. IT'S POSSIBLE TO ACCESS YOUR ACCOUNT VALUES WITHOUT INTERRUPTING THE GROWTH.

But with all of that said, there are unique financial strategies that allow you to use and access your account values without interrupting your compound growth. These strategies have been practiced by banks and wealthy people for decades. You can design a financial strategy, with my help or the help of a like-minded advisor, in which your accounts do not stop growing when you need to use the values you have accumulated.

Before we move on to our final financial truth, let's take a look in the next chapter at the big picture of what we've already learned.

SEVEN

SEEING THE BIG PICTURE

WE NOW HAVE uncovered nine financial truths. I want to list them again so we can take one more look at them all together. Then I will summarize them with one last financial truth.

FINANCIAL TRUTH #1:
Compound interest is one of the greatest tools for building wealth.

FINANCIAL TRUTH #2:
Compound interest stops compounding when a loss is experienced.

FINANCIAL TRUTH #3:
Compound interest stops compounding when a fee is charged to our account.

FINANCIAL TRUTH #4:
Compound interest stops compounding when taxes are paid on our gains.

FINANCIAL TRUTH #5:
Compound interest stops compounding when we use our own money.

FINANCIAL TRUTH #6:
A higher rate of return does not always result in more money.

FINANCIAL TRUTH #7:
Fees charged to our account are a guaranteed reduction in our account values.

FINANCIAL TRUTH #8:
We are not required to pay taxes on our gains, if we use specific strategies that are approved by the Internal Revenue Code.

FINANCIAL TRUTH #9:
Life interruptions do not have to stop our compounding growth. It's possible to access your account values without interrupting the growth.

These nine financial truths are the key to unlocking the power of compound interest. They enable a hypothetical calculation to become a reality in your life. And these nine truths can be summarized into one final financial truth.

FINANCIAL TRUTH #10:
DECREASING THE COSTS TO BUILD WEALTH HAVE A MUCH GREATER IMPACT THAN LOOKING FOR WAYS TO INCREASE THE RATE OF RETURN.

With so much focus on how to increase rates of return on our money, it's easy to forget the costs of investing. As I've demonstrated, decreasing the costs to build wealth has a huge impact on how our investments perform. We've all heard the proverb "A penny saved is a penny earned." That also applies here. A loss avoided is—in and of itself—a gain.

When I use the word *cost* in the context of investing, I mean much more than monetary costs like taxes and fees. I'm also referring to lost opportunity costs, such as when you withdraw money from your accounts to pay for life's interruptions. You saw in an earlier chapter how a 9.25% return quickly turns into 2.38%—after these costs are factored in. That's a difference of 6.87 percentage points.

Ask yourself this: Do you think it would be easier to reduce the costs of investing—or to increase your annual return by almost seven percentage points each and every year?

I can tell you from my own experience, it's far easier to reduce the costs of investing than to find a way to increase annual returns by seven percentage points to cover the costs associated with investing our money.

THERE'S STILL TIME!

I want to take a moment to encourage you. No matter where you are in life, time is still on your side. If you're in your twenties or thirties, you have the ability to start on the right financial path. That has immeasurable value.

If you are in your fifties or sixties, you still have plenty of time to turn things around to your benefit. With advances in medical technology, it's very likely a person in their sixties will live another 30 years. That's a long time! But even if it's just another 19 years, look at the difference 19 years made in the examples we've discussed.

GET THE WHOLE PICTURE

I also want to challenge you—to never again accept a prospectus, illustration, or projection that shows you uninterrupted compound interest. Demand the truth. Ask for numbers that contain the variables we've discussed. Ask for historical market returns that contain both the gains and the losses. Ask for fees to be factored into the numbers. Ask for taxes to be taken out of the account when there's a gain.

And make sure you're given a clear answer about the result of accessing your money in a time of need. Will a penalty be assessed? Is there a withdrawal or surrender charge? Will the growth stop on the money you have removed?

These are great questions to ask your advisor to make sure you are making a fully informed decision. I have financial software that allows all of these variable interruptions to be inserted in just a few minutes. It can be done.

LEARN THE WHOLE TRUTH

Keep pressing forward in your pursuit of the truth about how wealth really works. I hope this little book has helped you realize there are other financial vehicles you did not know existed. Maybe you've rejected certain vehicles in the past, but will now want to give them a fresh look.

Whatever the case may be, the knowledge you have today will help you only if you act on it. Today is the day the truth can set you free. Seize the day.

Look for upcoming books in The Other Side of the Coin series for more financial truths that can truly change your life.

DIVERSIFICATION: ANOTHER VARIABLE

THERE IS ANOTHER significant reason our account values don't grow at the same rate as the stock market. Strictly speaking this is not an interruption, and it's also a little more technical, so I will cover it in an appendix.

In this book, we looked solely at the *stock* market, specifically the S&P 500 Index. This means that in these examples, our money was 100% invested in stocks. How many people have only stocks in their portfolio? Very few. A traditional portfolio will have stocks, bonds, maybe mutual funds, and some cash. The percentages of these four will vary based on risk tolerance, age, and other variables, but having money spread out over these four categories is very typical. It's commonly referred to as *diversification*. Don't keep all your eggs in one basket, right?

Go ahead and grab your latest quarterly statement for your 401(K), IRA, or investment account. You probably have a pie chart in there that shows you the breakdown of your account's holdings.

Maybe you have 60% in stocks, 35% in bonds, and 5% in cash—or something along those lines.

The idea behind diversification is to help you weather the storm if the stock market tumbles. If you have bonds, so most advisors say, your entire account won't crash when the stock market does. (Bond positions delivered some of the only positive returns in 2008.) So having bonds in our portfolio sounds reasonable, doesn't it?

There are usually pros and cons to decisions, so what are the cons with using bonds to diversify against risk? The con in this example is a lower overall rate of return on your entire portfolio. Bonds may be safer than stocks, but they are known to have a much lower return. At least over the long haul. So the effect of adding bonds to your account mix is to reduce your account's overall rate of return.

This sounds like a catch-22. Without bonds, your account might be devastated by a crash in the stock market. With bonds, your return drops.

Look at the table below. This compares investing $100,000 with true, uninterrupted compound interest at 9.25%, against being fully invested in the S&P 500 Index, against a diversified portfolio.[10]

10   This hypothetical diversified portfolio is 60% stocks, 35% bonds, and 5% cash. The stock returns represent the total returns of the S&P 500 from 1997–2015, including dividends. The bond returns represent the total returns of the Barclays U.S. Aggregate Bond Index from 1997–2015.

Year	9.25% (True Compound Interest)	S&P 500 (Without Taxes or Fees)	Diversified (Without Taxes or Fees)
0	$100,000	$100,000	$100,000
1	$109,250	$133,360	$123,394
2	$119,356	$171,474	$149,598
3	$130,396	$207,552	$170,901
4	$142,458	$188,665	$164,381
5	$155,635	$166,233	$154,820
6	$170,031	$129,495	$137,915
7	$185,759	$166,648	$162,471
8	$202,942	$184,779	$175,843
9	$221,714	$193,852	$182,745
10	$242,222	$224,461	$203,770
11	$264,628	$236,784	$215,631
12	$289,106	$149,174	$166,658
13	$315,848	$188,645	$194,620
14	$345,064	$217,055	$216,664
15	$376,983	$221,635	$225,796
16	$411,854	$257,096	$250,771
17	$449,950	$340,370	$298,886
18	$491,571	$386,967	$332,197
19	**$537,041**	**$392,307**	**$335,923**

Notice that another $56,384 has been lost due to diversification. And this loss would be in addition to the other losses we have discussed: market losses, fees, taxes, and using our own money.

This doesn't mean that diversification is a bad thing we should avoid. There have been many hot debates over whether one should diversify, and I'd rather not jump into that debate here.

The point I want to highlight is that having bonds in your portfolio will most likely lower your account's overall return. I can use really simple math to illustrate this.

Let's say you invest $100,000 and want to earn 10% on that money the first year. This means your account would grow to $110,000. If you have 50% of your account in bonds, say earning 5%, that half of your account ($50,000) will earn $2,500 the first year. Because your goal is to earn $10,000, the other half of your portfolio, the $50,000 invested in stocks, will need to earn $7,500.

What rate of return is needed on that $50,000 to earn $7,500 in one year? The answer is 15%! So in this example, the stock portion of your account will have to produce incredible returns (much more than 10%) just to achieve an overall return of 10%.

This issue of diversification is yet *another* variable when it comes to investing. And sadly, this is yet another variable that is seldom fully explained to the hard-working people who are trying to save for retirement. To avoid yet another disappointment, make sure you get all the facts—and what they mean for your financial goals.

WILL DUFFY equips people with vital insights to make the most of their money. He's earned an enthusiastic following by helping people retire that didn't know they could, helping executives save money on taxes, putting young people on the path of becoming wealthy, and starting countless others on the path to financial freedom. Tirelessly teaching the whole truth about how wealth really works, Will enjoys the recognition of some of the top names in the financial services industry including his mentor, Ed Slott.

After graduating high school in Denver, Colorado, Will attended The Ohio State University. And Will received his Chartered Financial Consultant designation from The American College of Financial Services.

Will lives in Colorado with his wife and three children (and one on the way!). Please contact Will through his website:

WWW.VERITY.FINANCIAL

Made in the USA
Middletown, DE
07 July 2019